CAROL MAKENE

STOP SELF-SABOTAGE

Why people procrastinate and how to stop it

First edition

This book was professionally typeset on Reedsy.
Find out more at reedsy.com

This handbook, short enough, is dedicated to people who always have desired achievements but for any reason are not getting them yet.

1

Introduction

Nowadays time is going fast. It is the perception for many people in the world that, not only the velocity of events and technology are speeding up, but science has continuously been doing research and found days to be shorter.

In this order of ideas, it is important to make decisions and take action with less delay every time.

The question that comes to mind is, Why do some people achieve their goals and many others do not?

Procrastination is something that catches you and holds you, hostage, in a place of ease, even if it is not so comfortable, but it is the place of least effort. You need determination and discipline to beat it.

The idea of this handbook is to quickly find out why people procrastinate and how to overcome this conduct which stops success or halts any purpose, project, or objective in life.

2

What is Procrastination?

Procrastination is the action of postponing something. This delay could be unconscious or it could be voluntary despite knowing that there will be negative consequences for doing so.

In other words, procrastination is the action to take no action immediately or maybe never.

Are you a Procrastinator?

Postponing commitments as a lifestyle, avoiding responsibilities daily, choosing fun activities instead of work tasks, thinking there is a long period of time to solve any circumstance, and continually interrupting your work to chat with your friends, are key behaviors that indicate that you are a procrastinator.

Professional or Amateur?

It depends on how often or how delightful a postponement could be for you.

3

Why are you Procrastinating?

Throughout life, human beings tend to avoid making decisions and taking actions for different reasons and justify this evasion by looking for excuses that often become their reality. Usually, these excuses differ from the real reason for not taking action.

Unfortunately, procrastination becomes one of the most difficult habits to break. Leaving the comfort zone, even if we are not satisfied or happy, becomes difficult because we do not like to make an additional effort or face unknown things. In fact, it is really common to hear people saying:

"I have not had time for this"
"My children demand all my time"
"I do not have money enough for that"
"Next week I will do that"
"I am too tired right now, maybe later..."

But behind any excuse and postponement there may be another type of reason for not doing things:

Fear to fail

Fear of what people think about you

Fear of the unknown

A lot of effort

Leaving the comfort zone

Peer rejection

Laziness

Low self-confidence

Rebellion against the rules required by the processes

Perhaps because it is necessary to take a break from the fast pace of modern life…

So it is imperative to find what is stopping you from overcoming this impasse, otherwise, procrastination will take root in your life.

Let me tell you a story, that is not mine, related to what I said above

"There was a Pharaoh and a town infested by frogs. Then Pharaoh called Moses and Aaron and said to them: Pray to the Lord to remove the frogs from me and my people, and I will let your people go to offer sacrifice to the lord.

Moses said to Pharaoh: Deign to tell me when I should pray for you, for your servants and your people, so that the frogs are removed from you and your houses, and that they only remain in the river.

And he said: Tomorrow".

In addition to this story, it is well known that important characters in history have been great procrastinators.

The Dalai Lama, one of the most recognized spiritual leaders in the world, at one point in his life, was known for his inability to set things in motion. But, the Dalai Lama was not always motivated to go to work, and during his student time, he was reported to be quite lazy. He has even told himself that only when the going gets really tough will he start putting the work into his studies, leaving everything until the last minute. But since then he learned his lesson from him and used his experience to motivate others.

Bill Clinton, the former president, was famous for his inability to follow through on a project, and with the distractions of his female staff, it's easy to see where his attention lay. Time magazine, in 1994 while he was in power, published an article about his seeming laziness.

Leonardo Da Vinci, who is one of the most famous artists of all time, was as well famous for his procrastination, to the point that his benefactor had to threaten that he would not support him financially anymore to get him to be inspired and finish the work to which he had committed with. Mona Lisa, one of his best-known works, took 16 years to be completed and many of his works were incomplete.

Victor Hugo, one of the most famous writers, had trouble getting his works done, preferring to focus on anything other than his work. He struggled so much with his lack of focus that he opted to ask his servants to hide his clothes and not give them to him until he finished his workdays. Only then did he manage to finish his writings.

But this does not happen only in famous and recognized personalities. To go no further, let me share my story.

I was raised in a simple family, with good customs, very honest, and quite conformist. Used to let life bring the day to day without much effort and a great fear of undertaking new projects. However, I met a totally different man than I was used to and married him.

My husband, who has always been clear about his goals and has been very grounded in reality, is a man who could be called Hyperactive because it is very difficult for him to stay in one place and postpone the things he has to do, he remains constantly in motion and usually achieves his goals.

Keeping pace with him was challenging for me but it was quite exciting to see my life constantly growing and moving. Realizing that what I planned could be achieved and that the key was as simple as taking action. It was truly amazing since as I said before, I grew up in a very slow-paced household.

Unfortunately, my marriage ended and sometime later I met my current husband. An affectionate, homely, calm, and procrastinating man.

Yes, as crazy as this sounds, it is reality. The fast-paced and active life he previously led had come to an end. Now my life was in an environment that seemed infinite, that seemed to have all the time in the world and there was no rush at all. And it is where my struggle begins to continue achieving my goals, but it becomes difficult because there is a being that stops me with a lot of love. And he stops me to such an extent that I lose my strength and give up accepting that to keep my home I have to postpone my life.

I know this sounds like an excuse and maybe it is but I finally got used to procrastinating.

There is something very certain and it is that the longer you wait to take action, the more difficult it will be to achieve it.

However, the good news is that you can do it and here I will give you some tips to do it.

I could bring up many more recognized people in the history of mankind or just ordinary people, but that would delay the main objective of this book, which is to take action. So we are going to continue with a fundamental point to achieve our objective.

DEADLINE
50
45
1/5
10
15
20

4

Accepting Reality

Nobody likes to admit that they have a problem, something that does not allow them to achieve their tasks, that makes them unproductive, or simply does not let them move forward.

However, only accepting that we are more reactive than proactive and that there are things that are difficult for us to do and sometimes we postpone them indefinitely, or we only do them when there is no other option, is the way we begin to change the habit of postponing for the habit of action.

The first step is to accept that you are a procrastinator. Do not be afraid to accept it, be afraid not to accept it and continue the same. You can give all kinds of reasons to justify and deny yourself that you are not a procrastinator, but the only one who loses is yourself because you will not achieve going forward. For your peace of mind, you do not have to make it public. You just have to admit it to yourself and accept it in order to change it.

Secondly, do not stay with the guilt, feeling that you are a bad human being. What you have to do now is thank yourself for realizing that there was something in your life to improve and continue with the purpose of taking action.

Finally, you are not going to be frozen thinking that if well-known figures in the history of the world were procrastinators you can be too. Remember that all of them finally got over it and made it. They found a way to fulfill their commitments. Even if your task is accomplished it is not the best idea to postpone until the last minute, as this creates uncomfortable moments, causes stress to people around you, creates discomfort to your collaborators, or simply gives a negative image of yourself.

5

Stop Procrastination

I could suggest that you set an alarm every 30 minutes on your cell phone, with a high volume and a stunning sound, to remind you that you have duties and commitments to fulfill.

Imagine being daydreaming, playing video games, chatting with your friends, taking a nap, or just staring at the ceiling, when suddenly your loud alarm goes off reminding you to take action.

Fortunately, there are recognized techniques to work on your goals and you also need to do a lot of deep work changing habits, and doing a series of jobs with yourself.

6

Tips to avoid postponing

Think that sooner or later you will have to fulfill that task and it is better to do it at once and not have it pending. Many times when we have a pending task this is not something that interests us much, we try to avoid it as much as possible. As regulations, these tasks have a due date for their completion, we do them at the last minute or sometimes we do not finish them, which leads us to a failure in that process, either not achieving a goal, not passing a subject in school, not finishing a project at work, or not fulfilling something that we had proposed. This thing of having something pending does not let your energy flow to move forward either, it steals your energy and your focus on your goal. We know that there are things that we don't like to do and as usual we try to avoid them as much as possible, but if we want to move forward we will finally have to do them, so why bother longer instead of getting over this as soon as possible if we have to do it.

If you have a big task or goal, take a planogram and make sure you spend the scheduled time each day for this task. When you finish it you can give yourself a small reward for your achievement that day, until you finish it completely. Organize each task in the planogram and at the end of the day an activity that you enjoy. Start the day by reviewing the planogram and there should already be reflected in the time that you must finish the task, what steps to perform, and how to distribute the time. In addition, the activity that will be the reward and that will motivate you to complete the task must be written and highlighted.

Remember, draw the planogram on a piece of paper, and hopefully, write by hand the tasks and each point needed to accomplish them, and the rewards.

Every time we write with our own handwriting, we make what we write more personal and more of our own. It is like an extension of our thoughts linked through our arms and hands.

Evaluate the situations that can give you fear leading to procrastination. Look at the pros and cons of not taking action and you will probably find that procrastinating will bring worse consequences than facing a situation no matter how difficult it may be.

Get up every day with the firm purpose of doing something that you have been postponing. Whether it seems silly, like making a call to a friend, buying a new cell phone cable, or something as important as taking your pet to be vaccinated.

When you get up, look yourself in the mirror, assign yourself the task out loud, and tell yourself "today I'm going to do (the task you've postponed),

I trust you and I know you're going to do it today".

At the beginning of each week, make a list of the tasks that you have pending and a short plan of when you are going to carry out each one of them. In front of each task make a small box to put your check mark once you have done it.

At night, before going to bed, take a few minutes to check if you have completed your tasks and put the check mark on those that are already finished. If you fulfilled it, you will feel the satisfaction of having fulfilled your duty and of having fulfilled yourself. I assure you that that night will be very pleasant and you will rest your body, mind, and spirit.

7

Achieve your goals

There are recognized techniques to work on your goals and you also need to do a lot of deep work changing habits and doing a series of jobs with yourself.

One of the most recognized techniques is to make statements. It works as follows: You set yourself a goal, the one that you truly want to achieve, and you write it as if you had already fulfilled it, in the present tense, as if you were already living that, several times on different papers and you paste each paper with the written goal in the places that you always look, one on the bathroom mirror, one on the nightstand, one on your laptop, write it on your cell phone screen, and repeat this affirmation out loud first thing in the morning when you get up when you go to bed and every time you see your phrase written during the day.

Another technique is to change the negative to positive. When a negative thought comes to your mind, something like "I won't make it", immediately change it to a positive affirmation, "I am achieving what I set out to do".

The next technique is, to keep a positive attitude. If you spend your time focused on the fact that your goal is too big for you, that you don't know if you can achieve it in time, that perhaps it is better to give up than to make an effort, you will probably give up and put aside the dream you had. There will always be bumps along the way but you must be clear that a stumble is not the end but part of the journey.

The most valuable technique in my opinion is to feel in your gut the conviction that you are going to achieve what you want to achieve. You can declare it many times but you also have to visualize the moment in which you achieve your goal, how you are going to feel, where you are, what that place smells like, what sensations you are experiencing and that moment of experience is what you are going to do part of you day by day on the way to achieving that goal.

It is well known that to achieve your goals you must constantly work on them, strive, and often make very significant sacrifices, which is true. But all this becomes even more complex if you keep procrastinating and procrastinating instead of doing what you have to do.

First and foremost is knowing where you want to go and what you want to achieve.

Second, make an orderly plan of how to achieve your big goal. That how is what you will need to achieve it and what small goals you have to meet and when you have to meet them.

Consequently, you must always keep in mind the big goal, that it is important that it is clear and that every day when you get up you dedicate 60 seconds of your morning to mention your goal out loud.

Additionally, every morning when you get up and every night when you go to bed, look in the mirror and tell yourself that you believe in yourself, that you are a person capable of achieving your goals and overcoming every obstacle that may come your way.

It is also essential to stay focused on what you are going to achieve each day to reach your final goal.

And most important of all, Take Action!

8

Epilogue

The whole life unfolds around one word, Action.

The development of the world, technology, each stage lived, and each achievement of the human being is given by a chain of actions. Everything is movement, nothing is still forever and likewise, you must go with that law. You can't get stuck. You cannot remain static and go against the law of the universe.

You must not postpone life, you must overcome fears, obstacles, and laziness. You have to take action.

Stop self-sabotaging!

www.ingramcontent.com/pod-product-compliance
Lightning Source LLC
LaVergne TN
LVHW052115160826
845678LV00015B/3567

* 9 7 9 8 8 4 8 0 3 4 5 9 2 *